VEHICLES
ON THE JOB

CONSTRUCTION VEHICLES

BY **JANET SLINGERLAND**

NORWOOD HOUSE PRESS

Cover: Every busy construction site has many different vehicles working.

Norwood House Press
P.O. Box 316598
Chicago, Illinois 60631

For information regarding Norwood House Press, please visit our website at:
www.norwoodhousepress.com or call 866-565-2900.

PHOTO CREDITS: Cover: © Pro-syanov/iStockphoto; © Alexander Erdbeer/
Shutterstock Images, 4–5; © chaphot/Shutterstock Images, 7; © Designua/
Shutterstock Images, 20; © Girodjl/Shutterstock Images, 6; © Keith Srakocic/AP
Images, 8–9; © knapjames/iStockphoto, 21; © Oleksiy Maksymenko/ImageBroker/
Superstock, 11; © Pro-syanov/iStockphoto, 14–15; © Richard Thornton/Shutterstock
Images, 17; © Roman023_photography/Shutterstock Images, 13; © Universal
Images/Superstock, 19

LIBRARY OF CONGRESS CATALOGING-IN-PUBLICATION DATA

Names: Slingerland, Janet, author.
Title: Construction vehicles / by Janet Slingerland.
Description: Chicago, Illinois : Norwood House Press, [2018] | Series:
    Vehicles on the job | Includes bibliographical references and index.
Identifiers: LCCN 2018003245 (print) | LCCN 2018011784 (ebook) | ISBN
    9781684042265 (ebook) | ISBN 9781599539423 (hardcover : alk. paper)
Subjects: LCSH: Earthmoving machinery--Juvenile literature.
Classification: LCC TA725 (ebook) | LCC TA725 .S56 2018 (print) |
    DDC 621.8/6--dc23
LC record available at https://lccn.loc.gov/2018003245

312N—072018
Manufactured in the United States of America in North Mankato, Minnesota.

CONTENTS

CHAPTER 1

A Busy Site 5

CHAPTER 2

Goodbye, Old Building 9

CHAPTER 3

A Fresh Start 15

CHAPTER 4

Hello, New Building 18

GLOSSARY 22

FOR MORE INFORMATION 23

INDEX 24

ABOUT THE AUTHOR 24

Note: Words that are **bolded** in the text are defined in the glossary.

An excavator helps tear down an old building to get the site ready for a new one.

A BUSY SITE

Engines roar. Signals beep. People shout. Vehicles move in and out. A construction site is a loud and busy place.

An excavator is hard at work. It is helping take down an old building so a new one can go up.

The excavator has many parts! It has a long **boom**. At the end of the boom is a claw. Different types of claws do different jobs. The boom moves up. The claw grabs chunks off the building.

When that's finished, a bucket replaces the claw. The excavator is ready to dig. With the help of construction vehicles like this, a new building will soon appear!

Excavators come in many sizes so people can find the right tool for the job.

PARTS OF AN EXCAVATOR

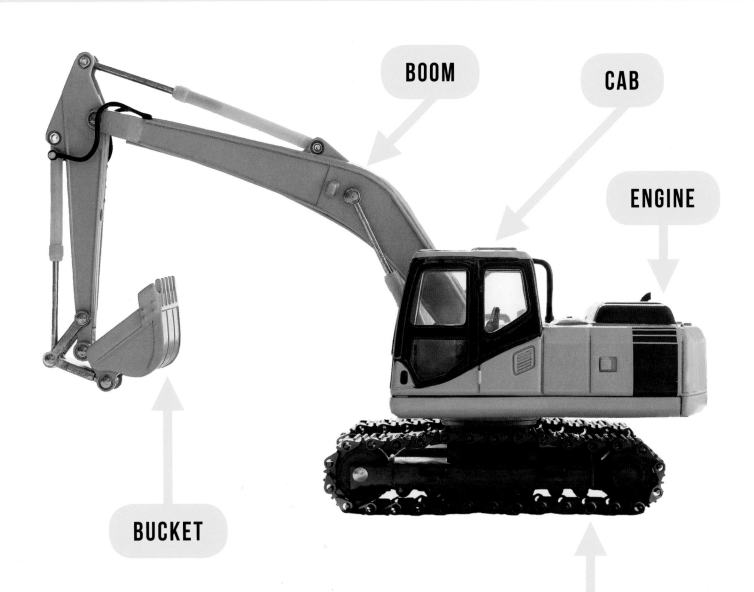

BOOM

CAB

ENGINE

BUCKET

TRACK

Some pieces from old buildings can be reused.

CHAPTER 2

GOODBYE, OLD BUILDING

A giant ball swings back. It swings forward. Smash! It crashes into the side of an old building.

Before a new building can go up, the old one has to come down. Sometimes, this work starts with a wrecking ball.

ON THE JOB: OPERATORS

Construction equipment operators control the machines used on construction sites. Schools called trade schools teach the skills operators need. Other workers learn on the job. Drivers of some machines need special licenses.

Operators move levers and push pedals. These controls drive the vehicle. Operators move booms and buckets. They swing wrecking balls and empty dump trucks. This all requires good hand-eye **coordination**.

This is a large, heavy, metal ball. It hangs on cables attached to a crane's boom. The crane may be on **tracks** or wheels.

The crane operator moves the boom. This swings the wrecking ball. The ball hits the building. This breaks the building into pieces. The operator must be careful to hit the target.

Next, an excavator may help. Different boom attachments give it different uses. Shears cut through metal. A grapple grabs chunks off the building.

Smaller machines start to work inside the building. A skid steer can often fit through doorways. This small

Skid steers can have different attachments for different jobs.

machine has arms in front of its **cab**. These arms usually hold a bucket attachment. This lets the skid steer scoop and lift things.

Other attachments help the skid steer tear down the building. Breakers let it break up a concrete floor. Shears help it cut through metal. Grapples let it pick up and sort **debris**.

Dump trucks come and go while the building is taken down. They haul away the pieces of the old building. A dump truck has a large bed behind its cab. This holds material and dumps it out.

The dump truck's bed lifts up to dump out what it is hauling.

A bulldozer may have tracks or large tires.

CHAPTER 3

A FRESH START

The old building is now gone. More construction vehicles help get the site ready for the new building.

A bulldozer is a large tractor that moves on tracks. A large blade sits in front of the cab. The operator lowers the blade. As the dozer moves, the blade moves what is in front of it. This evens out the earth the new building will sit on.

The site is ready for its **foundation**. An excavator uses its bucket to scoop out the earth. The operator follows the building plans. The foundation must be just right.

Now there is a pile of extra dirt on the site. A front-end loader moves in. This machine has a large scoop in front of the cab. The operator lowers the scoop and moves forward to scoop up the dirt. The operator lifts the scoop to dump the dirt into a dump truck. The dump truck hauls the dirt away so it can be reused somewhere else.

A front-end loader and a dump truck work together to remove extra material from a construction site.

CHAPTER 4

HELLO, NEW BUILDING

The site is level. The foundation is dug. It's time to build.

A concrete mixer moves in. This truck has a large spinning drum behind the cab. The drum spins, mixing the concrete while it moves to the building site. Once there, a **chute** connects to the drum. Workers point the chute so the concrete flows where it is needed.

Flatbed trucks carry materials. They haul beams that will make up the building. They even haul other vehicles.

Concrete may flow down a chute attached to the truck or be pumped through special hoses.

A flatbed truck might carry a forklift to a construction site. This small machine has fork-like prongs in front of its cab. The operator lowers the prongs to fit under a **pallet** of supplies. The prongs slide into the pallet. The operator raises the prongs to lift it. The forklift moves around the site to deliver the materials.

STEM AT WORK: PULLEYS

COMPOUND PULLEY

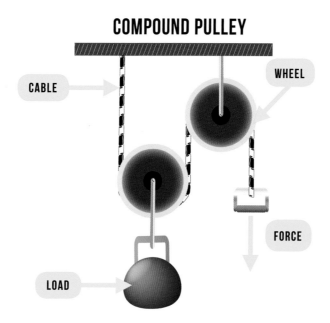

CABLE

WHEEL

FORCE

LOAD

Cranes lift heavy things. They use pulleys to help. A pulley is a simple machine. It is a cable slung over a wheel above a load.

We use **force** to lift a load. But a pulley changes the direction of the force. Instead of pulling up to lift the load, we pull down to lift the load. This makes the work easier.

Cranes use compound pulleys. A compound pulley adds a pulley above the load. This reduces the amount of force needed to lift the load.

As the building grows, cranes move in. They rise hundreds of feet in the air! They lift items to upper floors.

Finally, the building is finished. Workers and construction vehicles worked hard together to create a building. Now they will move on to the next job!

Cranes can lift anything from beams and flooring to wet concrete!

GLOSSARY

boom (BOOM): A long beam used to support or guide something being lifted.

cab (CAB): The covered area where the operator of a truck or other machine can sit or stand.

chute (SHOOT): A sloped channel down which things can flow.

coordination (koh-ord-ih-NAY-shun): The ability for things to work together.

debris (deh-BREE): The pieces left of something that has been broken or destroyed.

force (FOHRS): The strength or energy needed to move or lift an object.

foundation (fown-DAY-shuhn): The support on which a building sits.

pallet (PAL-let): A low, portable platform used for storing and moving materials.

tracks (TRAX): Two continuous belts on which a vehicle, such as a tank, moves.

FOR MORE INFORMATION

BOOKS

Arnold, Quinn M. *Bulldozers*. Mankato, MN: Creative, 2018. This book explores types of bulldozers and how they work.

Baumann, Anne-Sophie. *The Ultimate Construction Site Book*. San Francisco, CA: Twirl, 2014. This book includes detailed drawings and diagrams of construction vehicles and the buildings they help create.

Milton, Joyce. *Heavy-Duty Trucks*. New York: Random House, 2015. This nonfiction reader includes photographs and fun facts about big trucks.

WEBSITES

Bob the Builder
www.pbskids.org/bobthebuilder
This site includes activities, games, and videos related to tools and cartoon construction equipment.

The Great Picture Book of Construction Equipment
http://www.kenkenkikki.jp/pbe/index.html
This site has pictures of every type of construction equipment you'll find on a job site.

INDEX

B

boom, 5, 6, 10, 11

bucket, 6, 10, 12, 16

bulldozer, 15, 16

C

cab, 12, 15, 16, 18, 19

chute, 18

claw, 6

concrete mixer, 18

crane, 10, 20, 21

D

demolition, 5, 6, 9, 10, 11, 12

dump truck, 10, 12, 16

E

excavator, 5, 6, 11, 16

F

flatbed truck, 18, 19

forklift, 19

front-end loader, 16

G

grapple, 11, 12

L

license, 10

O

operator, 10, 15, 16, 19

P

pulley, 20

S

shears, 11, 12

skid steer, 11, 12

T

tracks, 10, 15

W

wheels, 10

wrecking ball, 9, 10

ABOUT THE AUTHOR

Before writing books, Janet Slingerland was an engineer, working on the computers that make things like telephones and airplanes work. She lives in New Jersey with her husband, three children, and a dog.